Sports Stars, Stats, and S

FOOTBALL STARS, STATS, AND STORIES

BY ELISE TOBLER

Enslow PUBLISHING

INVESTIGATE!

Please visit our website, www.enslow.com. For a free color catalog of all our high-quality books, call toll free 1-800-398-2504 or fax 1-877-980-4454.

Library of Congress Cataloging-in-Publication Data
Names: Tobler, Elise, 1970- author.
Title: Football stars, stats, and stories / Elise Tobler.
Description: Buffalo : Enslow Publishing, LLC, [2025] | Series: Sports Stars, Stats, and Stories | Includes bibliographical references and index.
Identifiers: LCCN 2024028830 (print) | LCCN 2024028831 (ebook) | ISBN 9781978542556 (lib. bdg.) | ISBN 9781978542549 (paperback) | ISBN 9781978542563 (ebook)
Subjects: LCSH: Football–Miscellanea–Juvenile literature. | Football–Statistics–Juvenile literature.
Classification: LCC GV950.7 .T63 2025 (print) | LCC GV950.7 (ebook) | DDC 796.332–dc23/eng/20240827
LC record available at https://lccn.loc.gov/2024028830
LC ebook record available at https://lccn.loc.gov/2024028831

Published in 2025 by
Enslow Publishing
2544 Clinton Street
Buffalo, NY 14224

First Edition

Designer: Andrea Davison-Bartolotta
Editor: Therese Shea

Photo credits: Cover, p. 1 (field) David Lee/Shutterstock.com; cover (flag) Mega Pixel/Shutterstock.com; cover, p. 1 (Mahomes) Darren Lee/CSM/Alamy Live News/Alamy Stock Photo; cover, p. 1 (football play) New Africa/Shutterstock.com; cover, p. 1 (ref) Brocreative/Shutterstock.com; series art (banners) WinWin artlab/Shutterstock.com; series art (fact box background) Adam Vilimek/Shutterstock.com; series art (jersey texture) Kwangmoozaa/Shutterstock.com; series art (tablet) Lemberg Vector studio/Shutterstock.com; p. 5 (bottom) antpkr/Shutterstock.com; pp. 5 (top), 24, 25 JoeSAPhotos/Shutterstock.com; pp. 6–7, 7 (inset), 20 (team) courtesy of Library of Congress; p. 8 (right) spatuletail/Shutterstock.com; p. 8 (left) Everett Collection/Shutterstock.com; p. 9 John Panella/Shutterstock.com; p. 11 (top) Marcus E Jones/Shutterstock.com; p. 11 (bottom) U.S. Navy photo by Mass Communication Specialist 2nd Class Todd Frantom/Released/Flickr.com; p. 12 (main) David Durochik/Associated Press; p. 12 (inset) jjaf/Shutterstock.com; pp. 13, 19 Zuma Press, Inc./Alamy Stock Photo; p. 14 Jeffrey Beall/ File:Thunder (horse mascot).JPG/Wikimedia Commons; p. 15 (top left) Joseph Sohm/Shutterstock.com; p. 15 (bottom right) Jamie Lamor Thompson/Shutterstock.com; p. 15 (bottom left) fitzcrittle/Shutterstock.com; p. 15 (top right) Jeff Bukowski/Shutterstock.com; p. 16 Debby Wong/Shutterstock.com; p. 17 Jonathan Kirn/Alamy Stock Photo; p. 18 Anthony Correia/Shutterstock.com; p. 20 (tv inset) File:Myhra-Field-Goal.jpg/Wikipedia.org; p. 20 (tv) Eric Glenn/Shutterstock.com; p. 21 AP Photo/Carl Viti; p. 23 (trophy) Wirestock Creators/Shutterstock.com; p. 23 (bottom) U.S. Air Force photo by Staff Sgt. Dakota Carter/DVIDS; pp. 23, 29 All-Pro Reels/Flickr.com; p. 26 Blulz60/iStockphoto.com; p. 27 April Visuals/Shutterstock.com; p. 28 Master1305/Shutterstock.com.

Printed in the United States of America

CPSIA compliance information: Batch #CW25ENS: For further information contact Enslow Publishing, at 1-800-398-2504.

CONTENTS

Words in the glossary appear in **bold** type the first time they are used in the text.

GREAT SPORT, GREAT RECORDS

Each season in the National Football League (NFL), teams and players set and break records of all kinds. The biggest fans love knowing the **statistics**, or stats, in their favorite sport.

Who ran for the most yards in their pro **career**? Emmitt Smith holds that record with 18,355 yards. (That's like running more than 183 football fields!) Who scored the most career touchdowns? That's Jerry Rice, with 208 (or 1,248 points)! Will anyone break these amazing records? Today's superstars are trying!

Get the Stats!

An American football field is 100 yards long between the goal lines.

Football is a team sport, with 11 players on defense and 11 on offense on the field.

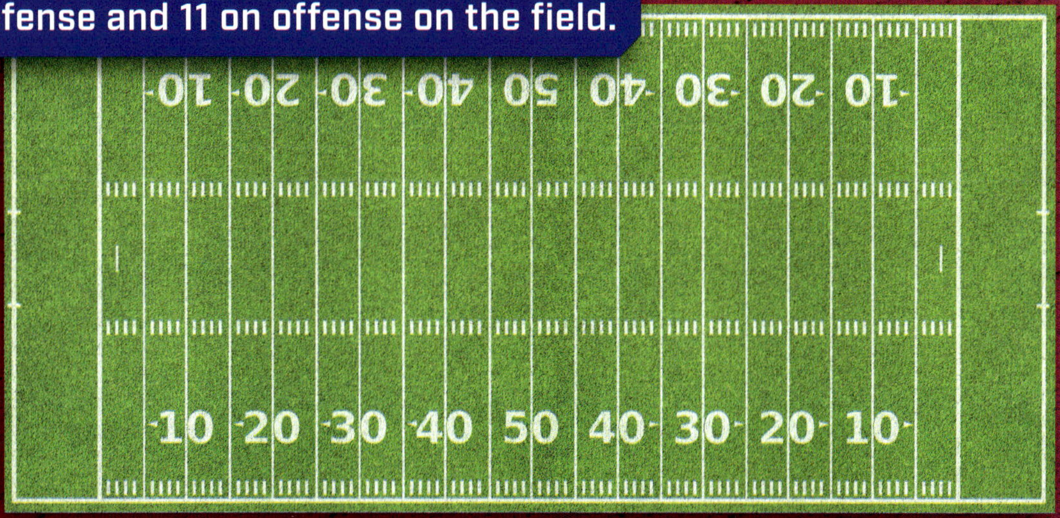

WHERE FOOTBALL STARTED

In the late 1800s, U.S. college **gridiron** football teams played a game that was more like soccer. After Harvard played a Canadian college that used **rugby** rules, the American team decided to use those rules too. Soon, other teams did as well. This made the game closer to the one we know today.

Canton, Ohio, now home to the Pro Football Hall of Fame, had one of the first pro teams, the Canton Bulldogs. The Bulldogs still hold the record for most wins in a row—25!

In 1920, the American Professional Football Association (today's NFL) started playing organized games. There were 14 teams in the league, compared to today's 32.

Get the Stats!

The NFL didn't require hard helmets until 1943.

MASSILLON VS. CANTON FOOTBALL GAME, 1906

POP GOES THE LEAGUE

Glenn "Pop" Warner (1871–1954) was a famous college football coach. During his 43-year career, he helped shape today's game. Some teams still use his plays. For example, Warner was the first coach to use the huddle, a kind of meeting on the field in which players talk about the next play.

POP WARNER

HUDDLE

Pop Warner Little Scholars, a youth football, cheer, and dance organization for young people, is named for Warner. Many NFL players got their start on Pop Warner teams, including quarterbacks Peyton Manning, Colin Kaepernick, and Andrew Luck.

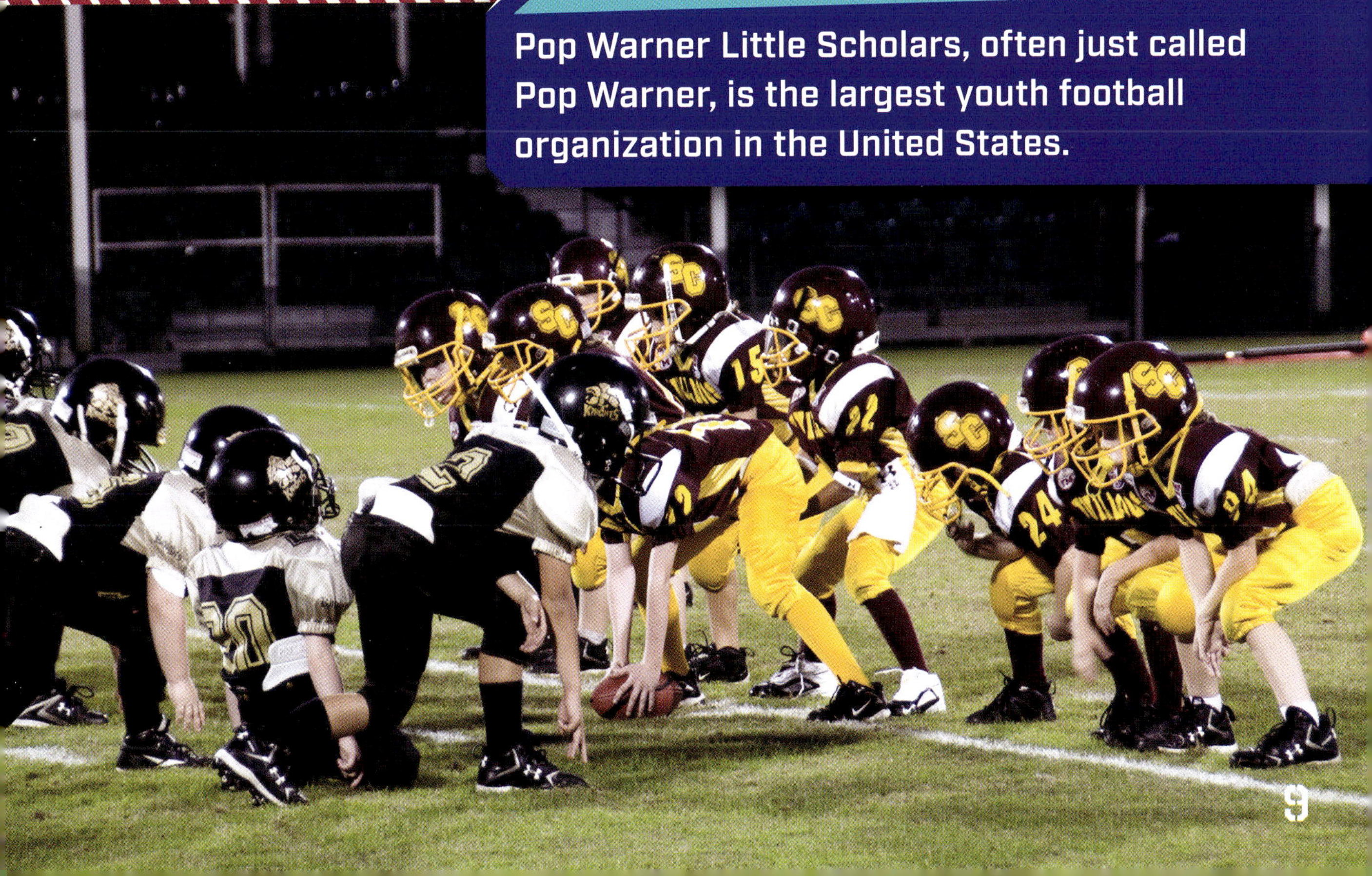

Pop Warner Little Scholars, often just called Pop Warner, is the largest youth football organization in the United States.

COLLEGE DAYS

Every year, the NFL **drafts** at least 224 players into the league. Most have played in college. College football is how the sport first became popular in the United States.

Like the NFL, college teams head to season-end "bowl" games if their records are good. The Rose Bowl in Pasadena, California, is one of the biggest games of the college season. So is the Army-Navy game, played between the U.S. Military Academy and the U.S. Naval Academy. This is one of the greatest **rivalries** in college football.

Get the Stats!

The first Army-Navy game was in 1890. In 2023, Navy led the rivalry with 62 wins to Army's 55.

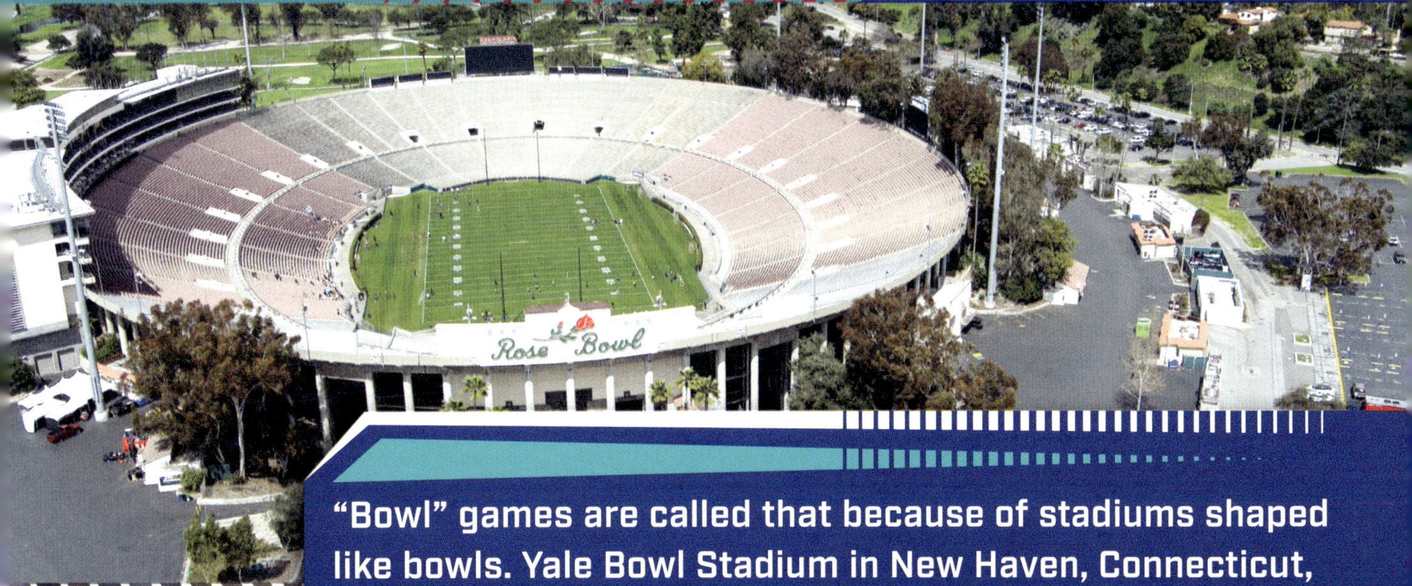

"Bowl" games are called that because of stadiums shaped like bowls. Yale Bowl Stadium in New Haven, Connecticut, inspired the building of the famous Rose Bowl Stadium.

ARMY VS. NAVY

HISTORIC NFL TEAMS

No NFL team had ever gone an entire season without losing a game before 1972. That year, the Miami Dolphins, with coach Don Shula, won all 14 games in the regular season. They went on to win Super Bowl VII (7) against the Washington Redskins (now, Commanders).

As of 2024, the 1972 Miami Dolphins are still the only NFL team to record a perfect, or no loss, season.

DON SHULA

Coached by Mike Ditka, the Chicago Bears lost just one game in 1985. They didn't even let the New York Giants or the Los Angeles Rams score in the playoffs! They easily won the Super Bowl against the New England Patriots, 46–10.

Get the Stats!

The 1985 Chicago Bears recorded a song called "The Super Bowl Shuffle" two months before the big game. It sold over 1 million copies!

In 2023, former players and coaches voted the 1985 Bears defense the best NFL defense ever. It allowed an average of just 12.4 points per game.

ON THE SIDELINES

Did you ever wonder why teams have **mascots**? They're supposed to **represent** the team and bring them luck. Some are people dressed up, such as Blitz, the Seattle Seahawk, and Billy Buffalo of the Bills. Some teams, including the Baltimore Ravens, have real animal mascots. The Denver Broncos have a horse named Thunder.

Sometimes, a team's fans are even more colorful than mascots! Green Bay Packers fans wear cheese hats. Los Angeles Rams fans wear hats with rams' horns sticking out, and Las Vegas Raiders fans dress like pirates.

Thunder and rider Ann Judge bring the game ball to the middle of the field.

Dressing up to cheer on your team is one way to show your team spirit.

GREATEST OF ALL TIME

Quarterback Tom Brady was a late draft pick by the New England Patriots in 2000. He went on to play 23 seasons in the NFL, 20 of them with the Patriots. His last three seasons were with the Tampa Bay Buccaneers. Brady was NFL Most Valuable Player (MVP) three times and won the Super Bowl seven times.

HOW GREAT WAS BRADY?

most regular season wins by a quarterback	251
most playoff wins by a quarterback	35
most fourth-quarter comebacks	46
most career passing touchdowns	649
most passes completed	7,753
most career passing yards	89,214
number of Super Bowls wins	7

Running back Walter Payton carried the ball for the Chicago Bears from 1975 to 1987. Payton was the NFL MVP and the NFL Offensive Player of the Year in 1977. He ran the ball for more than 1,000 yards in 10 different seasons.

Walter Payton won Super Bowl XX (20) with the Bears. The Walter Payton NFL Man of the Year Award is an honor given to a player who does great acts of charity on and off the football field.

Quarterback Peyton Manning played 18 years in the NFL. Manning started his NFL career with the Indianapolis Colts in 1998. In his first year, he set rookie, or first-year, records for completions, touchdowns, and passing yards. Manning spent his last four seasons with the Denver Broncos.

PEYTON'S CAREER HIGHLIGHTS

most NFL MVP awards	**2003, 2004, 2008, 2009, 2013**
Walter Payton Man of the Year	**2006**
most passing touchdowns in a season	**55**
most passing yards in a season	**5,477**
most touchdown passes in a game (tied)	**7**
career passing yards	**71,940**
number of Super Bowl wins	**2**

Jerry Rice was a wide receiver in the NFL for 20 years. He played with the San Francisco 49ers from 1985 to 2000 and finished his career with the Oakland Raiders and the Seattle Seahawks. He holds NFL records for receptions (1,549), receiving yards (22,895), and touchdowns (208).

As a wide receiver, Jerry Rice caught passes from the quarterback and ran with them. Rice holds a record for the most 1,000-yard receiving seasons, with 14.

GAMES TO REMEMBER

Some say the greatest game ever was the 1958 NFL **Championship** between the Baltimore Colts and the New York Giants. With seven seconds left, a Baltimore field goal tied up the close match, sending it into **sudden death** overtime. Baltimore won.

A 1982 game between the Stanford Cardinals and the California Golden Bears wins for craziest ending. A Stanford field goal put the Cardinals up by 1 point with four seconds left. Then, with Stanford fans celebrating too early on the field, the Golden Bears ran the kickoff back for a game-winning touchdown!

Get the Stats!

Many fans call the last play of the Stanford-California game "The Play." Kevin Moen, who made the final touchdown, said, "There were so many people on the field I couldn't tell when I crossed into the end zone."

The Stanford band celebrated on the field as the last play was happening.

SUPER BOWLS

Since 1967, football's biggest event has been the Super Bowl championship game. The winner of the National Football Conference (NFC) takes on the winner of the American Football Conference (AFC). The Super Bowl's winning team gets the Vince Lombardi Trophy, named for the famous Packers coach.

As of 2024, the Patriots have the most Super Bowl appearances with 11. The Patriots and the Pittsburgh Steelers are tied for most Super Bowl wins, with six. The Cleveland Browns, Detroit Lions, Houston Texans, and Jacksonville Jaguars haven't played in a Super Bowl.

Get the Stats!

In the 2023 Super Bowl, Jason Kelce (Philadelphia Eagles) and Travis Kelce (Kansas City Chiefs) made history as the first brothers to play in a Super Bowl against each other.

PATRICK MAHOMES

In 2024, the Kansas City Chiefs, led by quarterback Patrick Mahomes, won their third Super Bowl in five years.

VINCE LOMBARDI TROPHY

NOT JUST FOR BOYS

Women have played football since the late 1800s, soon after the sport began. Today, many high schools have flag football teams for young women, but tackle football is growing as a sport for women too.

Sam Gordon was 9 when she recorded 35 touchdowns and 65 tackles in her youth league. Later, she didn't have a league to play in—until she founded an all-girls youth tackle league in 2015, the first one. The Utah Girls Tackle Football League has more than 600 players. In 2017, Gordon received the NFL Game Changer Award.

Pop Warner Little Scholars reports about 2,500 girls take part in the organization's football teams.

No rule stops women from playing in the NFL. Some are trying to reach the top of the sport. Women have played—and scored—as kickers in college football. In 2023, Haley Van Voorhis, a **safety** for Shenandoah University in Virginia, became the first woman in **NCAA** history to play a non-kicking position.

In 2015, Sarah Thomas became the first full-time female **referee** in the NFL. She was also the first female referee in a college bowl game and in a Super Bowl. In 2021, Maia Chaka became the first Black female referee.

SARAH THOMAS

Get the Stats!

The Women's Football Alliance began in 2009 and currently has 60 teams. It's the biggest tackle football league for women.

Women are NFL team owners, scouts, and coaches too.

THE FUTURE OF FOOTBALL

Football has been the number-one favorite sport in the United States since 1972, according to the Gallup company's yearly poll. Super Bowl LVIII (58) in 2024 was the second most-watched TV event ever, after the first moon landing!

Every year, new players join Pop Warner teams and college teams. Women's football leagues are growing larger. The NFL draft pool of talent will grow larger too. Who will be the next big thing in football? It could be someone playing in a youth league right now. It could be you!

Even the best players in the NFL, such as Baltimore Ravens quarterback Lamar Jackson, were once rookies. Everyone starts the game in the same place.

Get the Stats!

Lamar Jackson won the 2023 NFL MVP award, his second. He has the NFL record for double-triples in the regular season, with 13. A double-triple is when a player records triple-digit yards, or 100 or more, in two stat groups, such as rushing yards and passing yards.

GLOSSARY

career: The whole amount of time someone spends at a job.

championship: Events that decide the overall winner of a sport or contest.

draft: Selecting a player from a pool of potential players entering a sports league.

gridiron: Describing a football field's appearance, with regularly marked parallel yard lines.

mascot: A person, animal, or object adopted by a group as a symbol.

NCAA: National Collegiate Athletic Association, the organization that controls college sports.

referee: An official who makes sure players follow the rules.

represent: To stand for.

rivalry: When a person or group try to be more successful than another over a long period of time.

rugby: A ball game in which two teams try to carry or kick a ball over the opponent's goal line. Forward passing isn't permitted.

safety: A football player who stands far back from the line of scrimmage and is responsible for stopping offensive players deeper into the field.

statistics: Information that can be related in numbers. "Stats" is the shortened form.

sudden death: Added playing time in a sport to break a tie in which the first team to score wins.

FOR MORE INFORMATION

BOOKS

Berglund, Bruce. *Football GOATs: The Greatest Athletes of All Time.* Mankato, MN: Capstone, 2022.

Buckley, James. *Big Book of WHO: Football.* Chicago, IL: Triumph Books, 2022.

Zweig, Eric. *It's a Numbers Game! Football.* Washington, DC: National Geographic, 2022.

WEBSITES

NFL 100 All-Time Team
www.nfl.com/100/all-time-team/
The NFL put together a list of the best players and coaches of all time.

NFL's Most Unbreakable Records
www.nfl.com/photos/nfl-s-most-unbreakable-records-0ap3000000415162
Check out this list of the 15 most unbreakable records in the National Football League.

Pop Warner Little Scholars
www.popwarner.com/Default.aspx?tabid=1476201
Find your local Pop Warner league and start playing football today!

INDEX